Rivering
The Poetry of Daphne Marlatt

Rivering
The Poetry of Daphne Marlatt

Selected
with an
introduction by
Susan Knutson
and an
afterword by
Daphne Marlatt

Wilfrid Laurier University Press acknowledges the support of the Canada Council for the Arts for our publishing program. We acknowledge the financial support of the Government of Canada through the Canada Book Fund for our publishing activities.

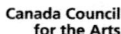

Library and Archives Canada Cataloguing in Publication

Marlatt, Daphne, 1942–
[Poems. Selections]
 Rivering : the poetry of Daphne Marlatt / selected by Susan Knutson ; with an introduction by Susan Knutson and an afterword by Daphne Marlatt.

(Laurier poetry series)
Includes bibliographical references.
Issued in print and electronic formats.
ISBN 978-1-77112-038-8 (pbk.).—ISBN 978-1-77112-040-1 (epub).—
ISBN 978-1-77112-039-5 (pdf)

 I. Knutson, Susan Lynne, editor of compilation   II. Title.   III. Title: Poetry of Daphne Marlatt.   IV. Series: Laurier poetry series

PS8576.A74A6 2014   C811'.54   C2014-900847-3
                                                                  C2014-900848-1

Cover painting: *Kickwillie Loop Kal Lake* ©River Lewis.

Cover and text design by Pam Woodland.

© 2014 Wilfrid Laurier University Press
Waterloo, Ontario, Canada
www.wlupress.wlu.ca

This book is printed on FSC recycled paper and is certified Ecologo. It is made from 100% post-consumer fibre, processed chlorine free, and manufactured using biogas energy.

Printed in Canada

Every reasonable effort has been made to acquire permission for copyright material used in this text, and to acknowledge all such indebtedness accurately. Any errors and omissions called to the publisher's attention will be corrected in future printings.

No part of this publication may be reproduced, stored in a retrieval system, or transmitted, in any form or by any means, without the prior written consent of the publisher or a licence from the Canadian Copyright Licensing Agency (Access Copyright). For an Access Copyright licence, visit http://www.accesscopyright.ca or call toll free to 1-800-893-5777.

At the mouth of the river, clans of the possible are gathering, the chinook, the coho rivering just offshore are us

from "Generation, generations at the mouth"

Table of Contents

Foreword, *Neil Besner* / ix
Biographical Note / xi
Introduction: Daphne Marlatt's Embodied Language Poetics, *Susan Knutson* / xiii

Street opera / 1
Coming in, who / 5
June near the river Clyst, Clust, clear. Clystmois this holding wet & clear / 6
Combe Martin, house martin, Martinmas, Saint Martin, martial swords & plowshares / 7
Avebury *awi-spek*, winged from buried (egg / 9
Litter. wreckage. salvage / 11
Ghost / 15
"Slave of the canneries" / 17
Winter / rice / tea strain / 19
Here / 22
This place full of contradiction / 23
Prairie / 24
Kore / 25
"Two women in a birth" / 26
"Imagin-a-nation in the heart of" / 27
There is a door / 28
Shrimping / 29
from *Mauve* / 30
Small print i / 31
Small print iii / 32
Small print v / 33

Booking passage / 34
In the current / 38
Generation, generations at the mouth / 40
Complicated / 42
Years ago / 43
Singing grass / 46
You remember / 49
Walking out / 52
Tree-song / 53
"Spectacular" / 55
To navigate / 57
Comes walking / 59
Marine, ah / 60
Through cloud / 61
Lift. step. drop. / 62

Afterword: Immediacies of Writing, *Daphne Marlatt* / 63
Acknowledgements / 67

Foreword

The Laurier Poetry Series began in 2004 with the appearance of *Before the First Word*, a volume of Lorna Crozier's poetry most ably edited by Winnipeg poet Catherine Hunter. Our hope was to bring contemporary Canadian poetry to its readers in a different way – by selecting thirty-five poems from across a poet's career, and by asking the editor and the poet to write an engaging and accessible introduction and afterword, respectively. Crozier and Hunter set the bar very high.

    I admit that one ambition I had in mind then – I still do – was to match the reach of the New Canadian Library. I imagined, hoped that what that series has done, mostly for Canadian fiction, the Laurier series would do for Canadian poetry. I hoped that in the high school and university classroom, poets would be better served by a volume that represented their work more widely than the usual anthology, with one or at best a few poems from each poet. And I hoped that more readers, old and new, beyond the classroom, maybe outside of Canada, would find these volumes appealing.

    Ten years later, with the twentieth volume just gone to press – and with the very recent and happy experience of using ten of the Laurier volumes, including Crozier's, in a fourth-year university class on contemporary Canadian poetry – a warm and vivid image arises in memory of poet Brian Henderson, then as now the Director of Wilfrid Laurier University Press, asking me over a beer on a hot June afternoon in 2002 in Toronto, at the Learneds, whether I might be interested in editing a series like this one. Then as now, I thought the idea was excellent. I didn't know if it would fly, though Brian's was, then as now, an inspired idea. A few more beers and an hour or so later, we agreed to give it a shot.

    Over this last (fast!) decade the dedicated group that Brian leads at WLUP – especially managing editor Rob Kohlmeier and his luminous team – have worked with an unimaginably wide range of poets and poetics. To what little I knew in 2004 about publishing, they have added their consummate and patient professionalism.

    What continues to inspire me about the Laurier Poetry Series, or LPS, has been its reception across the country. The love and art and passion and intimacy that twenty editors and twenty poets have brought to their volumes; the innumerable hours and conversations and meetings, the thousands of emails between and among poets and editors and Wilfrid Laurier; the generous reviews in the country's journals; the reception in classrooms and beyond: all of this eloquently speaks to the joyful proliferation of poetry in Canada today – and tomorrow. What a tremendous wealth of poets and readers we have here! What vital riches!

With each new volume, the Laurier Poetry Series hopes to continue to recognize the growing provenance of this wealth, the wide range of these riches. Our poets – and their readers – deserve nothing less.

– *Neil Besner*
General Editor

Biographical Note

Daphne Marlatt (née Buckle) was born in Melbourne, Australia, in 1942, spent her early childhood in Penang, Malaysia, and immigrated to Vancouver, Canada, in 1951 with her family. In 1964 she received her B.A. in English and Creative Writing at the University of British Columbia, where she studied poetry and poetics with Robert Creeley, Robert Duncan, and Charles Olson and was involved with the Tish group of poets. In 1968 she graduated from Indiana University with an M.A. in Comparative Literature. Her first book, *Frames of a Story*, appeared from Ryerson Press in 1968, followed by *leaf leaf/s* from Black Sparrow Press (Los Angeles) in 1969. She returned to Vancouver in 1971.

The subsequent years of her work were shaped by interest in the struggles of immigrants and the internment of Japanese Canadians during World War II. First with Maya Koizumi and then with Carole Itter, she collaborated on two aural histories, *Steveston Recollected* (1975) and *Opening Doors* (1979, 2011), and then with Robert Minden on *Steveston*, a long poem series with Minden's photographs (1974, 2001). Her novel *Ana Historic* (1997, 2013) also stemmed from this concern and from her interest in the history of her adopted city, first announced in *Vancouver Poems* (1972). This interest in the spirit of the city and its various historical periods continues in recent work, *The Given* (2008), awarded the Dorothy Livesay Poetry Prize, and *Liquidities: Vancouver Poems Then and Now* (2013). Much of her work is entwined with concern for the natural environment and for recognition of First Nations peoples and their living cultures rooted in this terrain.

Early on her work was marked by a feminist awareness (*Rings*, 1971) and a critique of imperialism (*How Hug a Stone*, 1983). In the 1980s she was active in helping to organize the 1983 Women and Words conference in Vancouver; initiating the 1988 Telling It conference while occupying the Ruth Wynn Woodward Chair of Women's Studies at Simon Fraser University; and co-founding the influential bilingual feminist journal *Tessera*. Her novels, *Ana Historic* (1988) and *Taken* (1996), together with poetic collaborations with Betsy Warland in *Double Negative* (1988) and *Two Women in a Birth* (1994), have been read as significant feminist texts. Her collection of essays, *Readings from the Labyrinth* (1998), documents that period of feminist literary thought and engagement. A later poetry collection, *This Tremor Love Is* (2001), presents varied facets of love in the context of a Buddhist sense of transiency.

Collaboration has been a significant aspect of both her editorial work and her writing. In the 1970s she co-founded a new prose magazine, *periodics*, and served on the editorial boards of several magazines, including *The Capilano Review*. Subsequent collaborations have led to a script for a short film, *The Portside*, directed by Aerlyn Weissman, which won the audience award at the 2009 Queer Film Festival; a contemporary Canadian Noh play *The Gull*, produced by Pangaea Arts and awarded the international 2008 Uchimura Naoya Prize; and, more recently, a Noh-inspired libretto for the chamber opera *Shadow Catch*, produced by Pro Musica in 2011.

At half a dozen universities across Canada she has taught literature, feminist studies, and creative writing and mentored younger writers as writer-in-residence. She has also mentored at the Banff Centre for the Arts Writing Studio, where she co-directed the Fiction/Narrative section from 2010 to 2012. Marlatt has authored and co-authored thirty books and chapbooks, several of which have appeared in subsequent editions. Her poetry has been collected in numerous anthologies; some of her work has been translated into Japanese, French, and Dutch. She is the recipient of two honorary doctorates as well as the Order of Canada, in 2005, and the George Woodcock Lifetime Achievement Award, in 2012. Daphne Marlatt continues living and writing in Vancouver.

Introduction: Daphne Marlatt's Embodied Language Poetics

In 1968, communities across this planet were in turmoil, and everywhere the arts were engaged and transformed.[1] In Vancouver, where radical poetics were ascendant, Daphne Marlatt filled in a questionnaire for her entry in *Contemporary Poets of the English Language*:

> Q: Periodicals to which you regularly or frequently contribute poetry?
> A: *Tish* (Vancouver), *Open Letter* (Victoria), *Odda Tala* (San Francisco), *Origin* (Kyoto)
> Q: Do you consider yourself primarily a poet? Other?
> A: Yes.
> Q: Do you recognize yourself as belonging to a particular "school" of poetry?
> A: No, though I do acknowledge a strong influence from the Black Mountain poets, & from Cid Corman/Louis Zukofsky, & frm Robert Duncan.

Marlatt also acknowledged Warren Tallman and Robert Creeley and the Poetry Conference of 1963 in Vancouver, where Charles Olson was present.[2] Then, in bold and telegraphic style, the young poet outlined the language poetics that would carry her through the next four decades of engagement with the world through and as language:

> first concern is with language, locus for event. That whatever "themes" exist are arrived at through language – recognized in that sense. Since whatever is known (expressible) is known in language, the poem becomes a way of recognizing or realizing the world, both inner & outer. What kind of ground we walk on, whose air we breathe. That the ecological principle in words forming one or many phrases runs whatever lies outside & forms also what we see – to say.... Verse (free verse, laid out with spaces indicating pauses) locates.[3]

In Marlatt's formulation, poetry locates the event and recognizes or realizes the world. "To locate" – from *locus*, Latin for place – means to discover, to place, or to "nose out." "To recognize" signifies re-cognition, and "to realize" means "to conceive vividly as real" or to "bring into concrete existence."[4] Marlatt's poetry-making is here declared to be of the kind that problematizes description or expression of the already known.[5] Rather, this poetics would discover – it would bring into being – "the world, both inner & outer."

Importantly, with respect to the inner world, Olson's teachings had recently drawn attention to the physiological concept of proprioception, arguing that it might be critical to poetry-making.[6] In a 1975 letter to Tallman, Marlatt

> balk[s] at that double sense of the self as *subject* of the writing: that is, the self is *not* what is written about though it *is* what is written out of. Subjective insofar as it *is* proprioceptive & the body is ground, yes, self transmits – but not, not the subject of the writing as what is written about, not so simply, only in that one cannot ever escape self because there is no other ground, & yet seek always what is "other" than self, that frighteningly small dominion, or to use Robin [Blaser]'s terms here, "What has been spoken is me."[7]

The doubled subject must remain dynamic, always seeking "what is 'other' than self," for the self is a "frighteningly small dominion." Yet "the body is ground."[8]

Early in her career, Marlatt refracted proprioceptive poetics through her lived experience as a woman, for instance in *Rings*, which deals with giving birth. In a 2008 interview, Heather Milne asks her about "continuities": "What are some of the threads that move across your work?":

> Well, to begin almost at the beginning for me, with the breath line and Charles Olson's approach to poetics, taking the body as a primary location for scoring the line on the page. I was very interested in that. And then I would look at Charles Olson's massive six-foot-six frame, a body that was nothing like what my body felt in its constant changing – how would I register my body on the page? And I became very interested in that whole area that, at that point, I felt was underdeveloped in writing: the physiological processes of women's bodies.... The rhythms were what interested me. And then with *Steveston* I started getting interested in the river delta as a female body, the way the river pours out to the sea and the tide swells into it and then ebbs again, all those cyclical rhythms felt very ecstatic and orgasmic to me. The long line I developed in *Steveston* was an attempt to carry that, and the meandering of the river.[9]

The poem "Litter. wreckage. salvage" attends to another side of what was called "the woman question," as can be seen in these lines from an early draft dated 1972: "If 'the woman is within,' / if that's her ground, what if, all the walls broke open suddenly, / Rain, Lightening, Light ..."[10] Although this poem was not published until 1991, in *Salvage*, it speaks to the situation of women in 1972, reflecting the insight that women would more and more implicate themselves in the political, public world rather than remaining in the home, long considered to be their "natural" place. Marlatt comments:

> Yes, ["Litter"] was earlier than *Steveston*, the book. i wrote it while i was participating in a writers' group that met regularly on York St. – Stan Persky, Glady (Maria now) Hindmarch, George Stanley, Brian Fawcett & others ...[11]

Marlatt has described her writing of this period as "early feminist, experientially rather than theoretically informed."[12] Feminist theory would come, however, and an important collection of that work was published in 1998.[13] Readers wishing to open up the rich dialogue between feminist writing theory and other pathways into radical poetics can trace Marlatt's early take on proprioception through to her mature and groundbreaking contributions to feminist theories of women's writing, for example in her most beautiful and well-known essay, "Musing with Mothertongue."

Marlatt's early period is finely covered in *Net Work: Selected Writing* (1980), edited by Fred Wah, whose essay introduces an audacious writer working in community with other teachers, poets, and novelists.[14] Companion to Wah's first important critical appraisal is the still-startling interview with George Bowering, "Given This Body," published in *Open Letter* in 1979.[15] The poems in *Rivering* pick up where *Net Work* ends, in something like their order of composition. However, as we have just seen with respect to "Litter. wreckage. salvage," strict chronology is complicated by Marlatt's method of working, which requires migrations between places, times, and texts.[16] Her methodology can be compared to photography, as she has suggested: the earlier poems are exposed to a second take and reread in the light of feminist reading and thought.[17]

The inner world of Daphne Marlatt's poetry is also inflected by the Buddhist practice which has long been a part of her life. *Rivering* closes with "Lift. step. drop," a walking meditation:

> In walking meditation, the effort is not just to slow down the body but to slow down the conceptual mind as well, its quick jumps from one association to the next. I found the effort itself was something like an attempt to short-circuit those connections, which of course keep sparking out of sheer habit. So each poem is an enactment of that process even as it tries to interrupt the seductiveness of language and its patterns – we think in words, so syntactic connection keeps leading us on, just as sound association does. The poems enact a sort of eavesdropping on this incessant internal chatter.[18]

Buddhism is also a presence in "Street opera," written and set in Penang, Malaysia, where Marlatt lived as a child and where she returned in July 1976, in the summer following the death of her mother. Illustrating the sparse line that characterized much of her earliest poetry, "Street opera" enters into Buddhist and Taoist thought: it is the Month of Hungry Ghosts, when passageways are opened between the realms of the living and the dead, and the suffering of the ghosts can be eased with rituals, musical theatre, and gifts.

> offer them food who
> come to devour
> the real
> banknotes, music, fruit
>
> we think we consume
>
> a fury of action they
> who pass beyond
> "actor & sufferer" both
> relinquish & remember

Recently rereading this poem, Marlatt herself was led to a discovery:

> amazed reading "Street opera" ... that line "actor & sufferer both" ... it's a perfect capsule definition of the *shite* in Noh – astonishing, because that was written in 1976 long before i thought i'd ever be writing a Noh play, though Dr. Shuichi Kato's marvellous class on Japanese literature in translation (undergraduate years at UBC), which first introduced me to Noh theatre, must have still been resonating in me.[19]

In the days that followed, she identified the source of "actor & sufferer" in the book that had accompanied her on that voyage "home":

> ha! i've just found my old copy of [Hannah] Arendt's *The Human Condition*, marked up in pencil from my reading it then, & i've located that phrase in the following:
>
> > Although everybody started his life by inserting himself into the human world through action and speech, nobody is the author or producer of his own life story. In other words, the stories, the results of action and speech, reveal an agent, but this agent is not an author or producer. Somebody began it and is its subject in the twofold sense of the word, namely, its actor and sufferer, but nobody is its author.[20]

Arendt's twofold sense of human agency here introduces another doubling of the subject as "actor & sufferer both," in which Marlatt recognizes the chief actor in traditional Japanese Noh theatre: the *shite*, sometimes translated as "the person who does."[21]

In Noh, intensely stylized poetry and dance tell the life story of the *shite*, and Marlatt has been drawn to this figure in some of her poetry and in her two recent poetic dramas.[22] *Shadow Catch*, a chamber opera, was created in collaboration with composers Dorothy Chang, Jennifer Butler, Farshid Samandari, and Benton Roark; directed by Colleen Lanki, it was produced by Pro Musica at Vancouver's Firehall Arts Centre in December, 2010. The action is set in *K'emk'émelay'* – the Squamish place name means "lots of maple trees." Today, that maple forest is in Vancouver, close to what is now Oppenheimer Park in the Downtown Eastside. There, a young runaway settles down under a tree, hoping not to be seen, and to rest; however, four characters appear in turn out of the past in order to tell him their stories. In this way, his sense of his surroundings is vastly complicated and he is released from a constricted focus on his own survival. The four characters with their stories resemble the Noh *shite*, and the effect of their stories on the listener also adapts Noh, where "the folding together of ... the sacred or other-worldly and the mundane, enlarges our view of what we live within, and releases us from a narrow focus on ... the materiality of our everyday life and the market-driven pace of the world we live in."[23] *Rivering* includes "Tree-song," sung by the spirit of the maple forest that once blanketed the shoreline.

Unlike *Shadow Catch*, *The Gull* was conceived and realized as a traditional Noh drama, insofar as that is possible in English. Produced in 2006 by Pangea Arts in collaboration with Noh masters Richard Emmert, Akira Matsui, and Hakuzan Kubo, it has been published by Talonbooks in a stunning bilingual (Japanese-English) edition with translation into Japanese by Toyoshi Yoshihara. The story takes us to the Japanese-Canadian families of Steveston in the years following the Second World War, as two orphaned sons prepare to make their way back up the coast to the salmon grounds their father once fished. With respect to *The Gull*, translation has moved both ways: Marlatt worked closely with Emmert and with Matsui to translate from Japanese into English the strict traditional musical, formal and poetic requirements of Noh, and then, subsequently, Yoshihara translated Marlatt's mostly-English script back into Japanese.

Marlatt's work with Noh reflects the fact that translation has been a passionate part of her writing life.[24] In the 1980s two small presses – nbj, from Montreal, and writing, from Vancouver – worked with her and with Nicole Brossard to create two bilingual (French-English) chapbooks of poetic

Introduction / xvii

transformance, translations that are readings, perceptions, and performance, and we are happy to include here Marlatt's *transformance* of one part of Brossard's "*Mauve*." In her essay "Translating *Mauve*" (1988), Marlatt comments: "paradoxically, it is through language which separates us that meaning flowers in the brain, seeping like a bruise from one mind to another in a transgression of limits. Translating *Mauve* became a remarkable performance of this process, a reading of the depths of the drift suggested by Nicole's minimal lines on the page."[25] Translation directs our focus to an other, a world outside, and to other cultures: it reaches across to "the outer world," the second term of Marlatt's 1968 pairing. It is both inner and outer, as she reminds us, for translation realizes a community of consciousness and a shared horizon.

Language as passage between distant or disparate human beings, and between human beings and the more-than-human world – these are drivers of Marlatt's poetics, and nowhere more than in her "great river poem," *Steveston*.[26] Created in collaboration with photographer and musician, Robert Minden, *Steveston* "gives accurate witness" to the terrible beauty of a one-time fishing village on the delta of the great Fraser River.[27] "Seeking to perceive it as it stands ..." (James Agee), reads the epigraph, and it is so:

> half moon, hot night. water seeping up, wetting
> island dirt. It's river, rank odour of river mud banks, the
> strait, the sea. That smell of night come lightly on the body of
> the earth's heat, full of the day.
>
> ("Moon")[28]

It is difficult to select from *Steveston*, for every detail demands recognition: all of the people, from First Nations and from around the world; the Pacific Ocean; the salmon (primordial); and the Fraser, "rivering urgency"[29] through the long lines and voices of the poems. "Ghost" and "Slave of the canneries" speak to the darker contexts of pervasive economic exploitation, internment and threatened destruction of the Japanese-Canadian community, the Second World War, "the extinction of open marsh by concrete; the burial of burial ground by corporate property."[30] "Ghost" recognizes the paradoxical place of death in the living ecosystem of our world:

> (ancestral: fertile as
> death: hello briar rose, blackberry & trumpet flower. All their faces
> lucent & warmlipt shining before your eyes: teachers, cabaret girls,
> longlegged American army wives you chauffeured, cared for, daughters,
> friends of your daughters, down thru the water smiles of easy girls,

caught, kore, in the black hole of your eye, yourself a ghost now of the natural world."[31]

Marlatt's poem telegraphs an ecological principle that was expressed prosaically, but still with beauty, by Charles Darwin 154 years ago:

> As buds give rise by growth to fresh buds, and these, if vigorous, branch out and overtop on all sides many a feebler branch, so by generation I believe it has been with the great Tree of Life, which fills with its dead and broken branches the crust of the earth, and covers the surface with its ever-branching and beautiful ramifications.[32]

Darwin, however, separated his human consciousness and language from the natural world that he studied, whereas Marlatt's embodied language poetics tease out and implicate the human in the intricate eco-economy of the river delta.

There is a compassionate and knowledge-seeking spirit in Marlatt's writing, an intelligence that goes "out to meet (recognize) an Otherness ... ," as an editor wrote to her of *Steveston* in 1974.[33] Warren Tallman saw it too, and in "Wonder Merchants" he offers this eloquent reading of her *Vancouver Poems* (1972): "drawn to places where the city is caught up in an almost brooding dream of itself, she dreams it back awake."[34] The poems in *Rivering* dream awake other voices and places: British Columbia's Okanagan and Kootenay Lake; Australia; Crete and the Greek island of Lesbos; Mio, Japan; and Avebury and Clystmois, England – "the nearest thing [she has] to a hereditary home."[35] Language, too, is dreamed awake as Marlatt researches and reaches back into the etymology of words, where ancestral meanings, though very much "other," are audible still.

In "Booking passage" and "In the current," language as passage translates across millennia or simply across the threshold of a door, to open into community and love without ambivalence. Marlatt celebrates love, and love between women – which not so long ago was mostly kept secret. "Litter. wreckage. salvage," "There is a door," "Two women in a birth," "Imagin-a-nation in the heart of" and "Walking" – all speak to the radical stepping forth of women and of lesbians onto the public stage. The three poems from *Touch to My Tongue* celebrate lesbian love in the full bright light of Petrarchan tradition, while "Prairie" and "Kore" appropriate one of the central myths of the Western world: Persephone climbs out of the hidden to brighten the beautiful living world. William Empson once wrote of the passages linking love to knowledge: the "truth-seeking idea seems fundamental to the European convention of love-poetry; love is always idealized as a source of knowledge not only of the other party but of oneself and of the world."[36] And, as Marlatt has insisted, if there is knowledge, there is language: "whatever is known (expressible) is known in language ... & forms also what we see – to say...." So, in "Small print," language struggles through technologies of print, fax, and telephone to reconnect with knowledge and with the world.

The possibility that language can bridge the consciousness of disparate, and even distrustful, human beings has motivated some of Marlatt's most significant political work, such as the 1988 conference that she organized while holding the Ruth Wynn Woodward Chair of Women's Studies at Simon Fraser University. "Telling It: Women and Language Across Cultures" brought together prominent First Nations, lesbian, and Asian-Canadian women writers, and the conference and the conference proceedings published by Press Gang were strong gestures of hope and clarity. The work that conference undertook – to bridge "the abyss" of "cultural difference" in order to realize our shared humanity – remains critical.[37] Marlatt, early and later in her career, has shown great leadership.

This essay has noted several paired ideas: inner/outer world, subject/subject, actor/sufferer, speaker/listener, and source/target language, in translation. In her afterword to this collection, Marlatt draws our attention to another of these, which is perhaps the most urgent for our times, and that is background/foreground. As long as the costs to the environment and to our full humanity remain in the background and fail to figure in the bottom line, we will not have the thoughtful and committed long-term engagement that we need in order to solve the problems our world faces today. Reading the darkest and perhaps the most powerful poem in this collection, "Comes walking," Marlatt's readers will decipher what is gone: "body as gift spurned grawk." *The Gull*, on the other hand, closes with a hopeful vision: "ocean joining here and there / one current circles through / torrents of disparate naming / wave on wave –".[38] "The geometry of human progress is an expanding circle of compassion," writes ecologist Carl Safina.[39] "One ocean washes all shores."[40] I thought of *The Gull* when I read Safina's words, and I thought of how literature, including Marlatt's *Steveston* and Joy Kogawa's novel *Obasan*, was critical in expanding peoples' consciousness and ultimately obtaining some redress for those whose lives had been damaged by the Japanese-Canadian internment during the Second World War, that awful outbreak of hate. It is my hope that this book, too, will play a part in healing our world, by serving as a "pocket Marlatt" for those who already love her work, and especially by introducing new readers to one of the best poets of our time.

– *Susan Knutson*

Notes

1. In 1968, students in Paris led their country to a general strike, and similar events took place in Senegal; China underwent the Cultural Revolution; the Beatles went to India and returned with the message of enlightenment and peace; in Czechoslovakia, the Prague Spring was met in August by Soviet-bloc tanks; the Chilean people prepared to launch their original path to socialism; anti-racist protesters occupied the computer centre at Sir George Williams University in Montreal for 110 days; Americans were transformed forever by the civil rights movement, the anti-war movement, and the assassinations of Robert F. Kennedy and Martin Luther King, Jr....
2. See Warren Tallman, "Wonder Merchants: Modernist Poetry in Vancouver during the 1960's," *boundary* 2, 3.1 (Autumn 1974): 57–90.
3. Questionnaire for Marlatt's entry in *Contemporary Poets of the English Language: An International Who's Who in Poetry* (London: St. James Press), from Library and Archives Canada, Daphne Marlatt Collection, Professional Correspondence, 15 February 1963–28 June 1973, Accession 1985–88, Box 7, File 7.
4. These quoted definitions and the synonym "to nose out" are taken from the Merriam-Webster Dictionary iPhone application, 5 September 2013.
5. Poetics, poem, etc., derive from *poiein*, Classical Greek meaning to make, to create.
6. Charles Olson, *Additional Prose: A Bibliography on America, Proprioception & Other Notes & Essays* (Bolinas: Four Seasons, 1974).
7. Letter to Warren Tallman, 13 February 1975, Library and Archives Canada, Daphne Marlatt Collection, Correspondence, file "Warren Tallman," LUS-0119 Accession 1985–1988, Box 6, File 11.
8. For another view on proprioceptive subjectivity, see Miriam Nichols, "Subjects of Experience: Post-cognitive Subjectivity in the Work of bpNichol and Daphne Marlatt," *Studies in Canadian Literature/Études en littérature canadienne* 25.2 (2000), 108–30.
9. Interview with Heather Milne, *Prismatic Publics: Innovative Canadian Women's Poetry and Poetics* (Toronto: Coach House Books, 2009), 244–45.
10. "Steveston. Support? Fish.," dated May–June 1972. Early draft of "Litter. wreckage. salvage," from Library and Archives Canada, Daphne Marlatt Collection, Box 14, file 9, Accession 1985–88.
11. Email correspondence, 23 August 2013.
12. Email correspondence, 23 August 2013.
13. *Readings from the Labyrinth*, ed. Smaro Kamboureli (Edmonton: NeWest, 1998).
14. Fred Wah, "Introduction," in Daphne Marlatt, *Net Work: Selected Writing* (Talonbooks, 1980), 7–21.
15. George Bowering, "Given This Body: An Interview with Daphne Marlatt, *Open Letter* 4.3 (Spring 1979): 32–88.
16. See Daphne Marlatt, *At the River's Mouth: Writing Migrations* (Nanaimo: Institute for Coastal Research, 2009).
17. Daphne Marlatt, "Foreword," *Salvage* (Red Deer: Red Deer College Press, 1991), 9. With respect to her complex chronologies, Marlatt writes:

> Some poems were written a decade or two before they found their way, revised, into a book in the company of related poems and therefore concerns from the

same period (sections of *Salvage*, *This Tremor Love Is* and *Liquidities*). Some series appeared as chapbooks, in a journal, or as small books and then were collected later with other works ("Month of Hungry Ghosts" in *Ghost Works*; "Here and There" in *This Tremor Love Is*; *Mauve* and *Character/Jeu des lettres* separate "transformance" chapbooks with Nicole Brossard, as "Acts of Passage" in *Salvage*; "Touch to my Tongue" in *Two Women in a Birth* with Betsy Warland). Some poems turned out to be the beginning of a series and were republished, somewhat revised, with the series they initiated (*Seven Glass Bowls*, which was a chapbook, became the overture section of *The Given*; "Booking passage" first collected in *Salvage* became the opening poem of the series "Sea Shining Between" in *This Tremor Love Is*)." (Email correspondence, 28 July 2013)

18 Interview with Heather Milne, *Prismatic Publics*, 250.
19 Email correspondence, 16 August 2013.
20 Hannah Arendt, *The Human Condition* (Chicago: U of Chicago P, 1958), 184.
21 *On the Art of the Nō: The Major Treatises of Zeami*, translated by J. Thomas Rimer and Yamazaki Masakazu (Princeton, NJ: Princeton UP, 1984), 268.
22 The *sh'te* also appears in "Wet fur wavers," *Liquidities: Vancouver Poems Then and Now* (Vancouver: Talonbooks, 2013), 5.
23 Daphne Marlatt, "Introduction," *The Gull*, by Daphne Marlatt with Japanese translation by Toyoshi Yoshihara, Preface by Richard Emmert (Vancouver: Talonbooks, 2009), 30.
24 Marlatt's M.A. thesis in Comparative Literature from Indiana University is a translation of poems from Francis Ponge, "Le Parti Pris des Choses" (unpublished). See also "Conversations with Readers: An Interview with Daphne Marlatt," by Beverley Curran and Mitoko Hirabyashi, *Studies in Canadian Literature/Études en littérature canadienne* 24.1 (1999): 109–23.
25 Daphne Marlatt, "Translating *Mauve*," *Readings from the Labyrinth*, ed. Smaro Kamboureli (Edmonton: NeWest, 1998), 72.
26 Warren Tallman, from a postcard (hand-delivered?) to Marlatt, dated Friday, 14 November 1980, Library and Archives Canada, Daphne Marlatt Collection, Professional Correspondence, 15 February 1963–28 June 1973, Accession 1985–88. Box 7, File 7.
27 I am citing a memorable passage from Marlatt's interview with George Bowering, "Given This Body": "I take it that a writer's job is to continue to give accurate witness of what's happening. One person isn't going to change what Marathon Realty is doing, what the CPR is doing.... You cannot change the world. You can change consciousness, & language is intimately tied up with consciousness. That's our true field of action, is language, as poets. And all you can do is to insist on the seeing as it's evidenced & manifested in the language. In an accurate use of language." *Open Letter* 4.3 (1979): 82, cited in Wah, 13.
28 Daphne Marlatt (poems) and Robert Minden (photographs), *Steveston* (Vancouver: Ronsdale Press, 2001), 17.
29 "Pour, pour," Marlatt and Minden, 15.
30 "Ghost," Marlatt and Minden, 51.
31 "Ghost," Marlatt and Minden, 52.
32 Charles Darwin, *The Origin of Species* (New York: Modern Library, 1998), 171.

33 Letter from Carl (no last name), dated 22 April 1974, Library and Archives Canada, Daphne Marlatt Collection, Professional Correspondence February 1974–December 1977, Box 7, File 8. Accession 1985–88.
34 Warren Tallman, from "Wonder Merchants," quoted in Marlatt's letter to Tallman, Library and Archives Canada, Daphne Marlatt Collection, Correspondence, file "Warren Tallman," LUS-0119 Accession 1985–1988, Box 6, File 11.
35 Daphne Marlatt, *How Hug a Stone* (Winnipeg: Turnstone Press, 1983), 24.
36 William Empson, *Some Versions of Pastoral* (London: Chatto & Windus, 1950), 135.
37 Daphne Marlatt, "Introduction: Meeting on Fractured Margins," *Telling It: Women and Language Across Cultures,* ed. Telling It Book Collective: Sky Lee, Lee Maracle, Daphne Marlatt, and Betsy Warland (Vancouver: Press Gang), 1990, 18.
38 *The Gull*, 73.
39 Carl Safina, *The View from Lazy Point: A Natural Year in an Unnatural World* (New York: Picador, 2011), 3.
40 Safina, 10.

Street opera

      (works, or
      words & deeds

      "the funniest story he told
      was of going to see *Hamlet*
      done as a Chinese opera"

satay
buah
mee goreng

these populous
night stalls
already existing
web

action
acts into

street
play

ཇ

godstick
dragon in an
old man's
sight

sharpens
all night

burnt paws
ashen ears
hear

it is 'seeing'
see

memory smoke

  ≥

wayang a
        way in
              no
shadow play
but neon, new on
the old

     acts

*can be told as
a story …* bios

 anyone's
 robe & drums

  ≥

the solitary hero
in his cups
jumps up

        challenged

        god comes, that
        audient

here
the act
enacts

here in the
din of the street
eating goes on
acting, speaking
heedless of all that
imitation

❧

satay cups array
god's house fruit heaps
this full moon night

        month of hungry
        ghosts

'life' invites

❧

offer them food who
come to devour
the real
banknotes, music, fruit

we think we consume

a fury of action they
who pass beyond
actor and *sufferer* both
relinquish & remember

ଈ

night stalls

satay, buah

mee goreng

relics
we transform

acting into

Coming in, who

    used to live here, used to
    the sweep of *kabun's* broom
    edge of a tideline morning used
    to run her energy along, alone
    exulting in birdsong, liquid
    trills, squawks

              the long
    reversible arc of his arm
    swept up grass, not up, around
    a kind of sortilege, *kabun*
    at the bottom of the garden, not
    looking up at the under
    side of sky, in the easy
    sweep of his arm, the long
    advance of noon, a tide

    poured through his broom
    she ran, through crests of song
    wave on wave, recede, while the broom
    continues its faroff rush, like surf
    coming in, she's gone

June near the river Clyst, Clust, clear.
Clystmois this holding wet & clear.

    it's haysel, haymaking time, "Sweet an' dry an' green as't should be, An' full o' seed an' Jeune flowers." tedding & cocking going on, shaking turning, spreading. haytrucks go lorries lumbering by these twisty lanes lined high with hedgerow, no seeing over, cow parsley, stinging nettles, campion, "day's eyes" & snails all colours coiled in their leaf byways. Jeune the young, green June delayed by rain. June, why do you punish me? "Take heede to the weather, the wind, and the skie." indeed, make hay while the sun shines you write, while the moon is on the wane. he wanes, my son redeyed & watery, phlegmatic in the face of *phleum pratense*, grass of the meadow, timothy spikes erect a masculine given name, god honouring. not her who is cut, full of young vigour, from the living book, from the play of light & shadow, nothing less than herb-of-grace, rue i find, there with the queen's pinks in the clock that is a garden.

Combe Martin, house martin, Martinmas, Saint Martin, martial swords & plowshares

this earth hospitable, *comfortably furnished. you can sit quietly listening to the movement of a nearby trout stream at the bottom of the garden.* at the bottom of Combe Martin. *steep cliffs, ideal for rambles.* coves with caves, slits, & what lies buried, treasure i told him, *trouvaille* of words rustling, seaweed, looking for minnows & crabs in tidal pools the rocks have caught back from the sea. in sandals, *sandalie,* the shoe of a Lydian god i buy him in a shop on High Street full of boxes. no cape, nothing else to change into in the phone kiosk.

nowhere to fly to but here, where even the grass makes him sneeze, June the worst month for pollen count. happiest in the Lucky Penny counting hits or testing quickness of eye against sci fi enemy bombers in Japanese computer games. divine wind recycled (on & on). while in Chatham they sing the Navy Blues, *getting rid of us at a high rate of knots* (outmoded). Nott planning to plug the Faroe gap with *nuclear-powered killer submarines & radar-equipped reconnaissance aircraft.* (getting rid of us.) while here small boats chug out to sea in the mist with a boatload of eyes, no sign of fish, a shark she said, lashed bleeding to the post on the beach in old revenge.

postwar turned prewar words return, swallows in the light: ices & Flook (luck invisible), chip shops spawning B & Bs, prim Ellesmere & Frittiscombe, Redlap, Merrymeet pristine even. *oldfashioned comfort is the rule. she brought us tea in the evening.* her husband a member of the Auxiliary Coast Guard sees what the Concorde does to the wind, flying overhead as it passes its twin from Bristol, wind rushing in to fill the vacuum of their passing, split & blown in 2 opposite directions at once. this is the image of the end, my landlady says, *wars & the rumour of wars. having forgot the sign of the fish,* she says, the, the, pointing to fix us in forever, how the meek shall inherit the earth meaning uncorrupt this body, even now *it is written, Our flesh shall slumber in the ground/ Till the last trumpets joyful sound* – sounding Creeks & Loverings & Berrys buried deep in small earth mounds, tombs, tumescent upthrust womb waiting.

& in owl light, twi-light, listen – where is my grandmother hiding out, cooking fish kedgeree off High Street? setting her foot with its golfing shoe untied on a sunny stone? look, Giggi, 2 snakes sleeping together. o my dear, she whispered, jumping back, o more than luck – grace, wingtip, brushed now by it in its turning. what does a child know? not *The Truth That Leads to Eternal Life*, my landlady handing it to me gift-wrapped. not there the light, flash, buried deep & inarticulate as earth.

perched on the rocks, birdlike, picking over small life in tidal pools, dead crabs floating by, or live & gone from the hand, i see my ghostly child in him, not gone & not quite him, as she in me, mother, grandmother, grand, full grown we stand in, not for. that earth takes back what is given, *ghos-ti*, hostly & hostile at once. *guests will be provided with a hot water bottle*, immaculately shining bath, long boat, long barrow at the end of the day's rambles.

Avebury *awi-spek*, winged from buried (egg

nose stuffed eyes holes in the chalk ridge of sinal bones rushed down back roads' upland grass wind weaving snakelike through. old English words: the land, the land, man's life *like the life of cereals.* woman's too.

bring to this place the line of a life (palm says it), motive in currents of changing weather, angst, cold for this time of year –

& small, toy pistol in one hand, cupped, & sheltered by the pelvic thrust of rock, jumps, gotcha mom!

                                              as if to fix it (sine), that jubilant ego in the face of stone, of wind flocking grey wethers *still gathered like* (but not the same, not these) sarsens now in place, immutable from long time back. & front, weathered yes, in folds acquiring character we read in, clothed & prickling now along the hairless spine, a line meeting a circle, two in one so huge (small hill) barely visible at grass view, red windbreaker fleck a sea of green & climb some moat in his imagination scaled he calls me to: come & get me,

the, all-powerful tickle, gulp, wriggle gulping in the whole world hugged in ecstatic limit, breath's. nothing still, no duration now (a line) creeps through fields of (waves of) renewed green, cloud, light.

what was it they got? craniums & long bones in long barrows, construction tools from 4000 years back, *antler picks, rakes, & some ox shoulderblade shovels.* what perspective from that elevation? *matrix of*

chalk block walls arranged in the pattern of a spider's web around & over a mound of turves, *grass still pliable though brown in colour ... beetles ... flying ants with their wings* showed them buried late July of 2660 B.C. why?

the line hypothesized druid lore (in Christian times), today a collective need to endure winter to spring, when *from his knoll…/ the Serpent will come from his hole/ on the Brown Day of Bride*, singing wave on wave emerging – & at centre, earth, only earth.

narrative is a strategy for survival. so it goes – transformative sinuous sentence emerging even circular, cyclic Avebury, April-May leaps *winged* from *buried.* sheds lives, laps, folds, these identities, sine: fold of a garment/ chord of an arc (active misreading). writing in monumental stones, open, not even capstone or sill, to sky (-change). *she lives* stands for nothing but this longstanding matter in the grass, settled hunks of mother crust, early Tertiary, bearing rootholes of palms. they bring us up, in among stone-folds, to date: the enfolded present waits for us to have done with hiding-&-seeking terrors, territories, our obsession with the end of things.

how hug a stone (mother) except nose in to lithic fold, the old slow pulse beyond word become, under flesh, mutter of stone, *stane, steiing* power.

Litter. wreckage. salvage

                                  below water level, behind – the dyke
a road now, back of the wharves, boats, empty sunday / spring, left
with the nets and houses left to dry rot, must, the slow accretion of
months as horsetail heads rear out of asexual earth of abandoned
gardens brambled

Steveston:
                   your women are invisible, your men all gone.

except for a few boats: hey, his spring salmon net's wet. how much
you got, Ned? a bucket. thin smile his pride will scarcely allow. WE –
got how much you say, Chuck? (pups at the old sea dog.) you stay
away with your bucket!

staying, straying in their individual houses women swim in long
slow gleams between blinds, day incessant with its little hooks, its
schemes inconsequential finally. they do not look at Star Camp, at
the company houses broke and broken open – litter of two-by-fours,
old shingles, bits of plywood forming/ doors torn off their hinges,
glass, glass remains of what transparent walls. occasional boot, the
wreckage of daffodils someone planted, someone thought to haul in
a bucket ... what matters, mattered once has seeped away. like fluid
from a cell, except she keep her walls intact, her tidal pool the small
things of her concern still swim alive alive-oh –

                                      ès.

fear of the marketplace, of going outdoors. fear of public places,
crowds, of leaving home. *the phobia of every day.* she trembles like a
leaf, has jelly legs. her stomach is a churn, fear stirring her into
separate parts: the whip of the superego, cowering ego, lack of will.

imagine opening your front door and standing on the step. how strong is your fear? relax, take a deep breath. imagine walking down the path to your gate. how strong is your fear now? relax. imagine opening the gate ...

i want to imagine being in my element she said.

〜

fish. paper. (value.) fish. paper. (words, work out towards ...) an accumulation of desires unbought, nothing in this world can pay for. i want to walk down the street as if i had the right to be there, as if it were not their construction site and stoop, slipping the net of their casting eyes, slipping the net of their market price. the street belongs to the men who live *outside*, whose small acts accrete (concrete) unspoken claim, a territory that cannot be trespassed except you hurry through, for loitering indicates a desire to be caught,

  or caught already prostitute, destitute, alcoholic, the street is where you swim for smaller fish,

      hey you! someone fishing for, hey where yah goin? that kick in the head recognition is, you! something other than fish, flesh, drowned in the tideline of the unemployable left on stone planters the city removes.

      whose foot of cement *is* this?

i go fishing too, to bridge that gap i let my line down into the powerless depths we flounder in where the will (to capitalize on things) stands on the opposite side of the street, having made this town, having marked it NO TRESPASSING NO LOITERING. no defenses in the smell of beer the private walls come down, light-fingered, airy as their harmonica, two young men sprawled in the heat and the young woman with them, flaunting her being there free, she thinks, for free –

12 / *Rivering*

fish that escape my line in the swift and surge the street my feet
keep carrying me adrift ... letting my line fall into the blank, the
mute, defences breached she's letting her want out there where
i am, beached with their receding ebb.

ə

coping with the world outside. she copes with this and that all
day long inside. a successful applicant must be able to cope.
she doesn't contend or strive – her struggle is within.

i can't take the bus is the same as i won't take the bus. a failure of
will. she says they were staring at her and what would she do without
the right change or forgetting to get the transfer when she got on, they
stared when he refused, they thought she was dumb. what attaches her
to the world? is what repels: the fear of being caught, caught out,
caught without –

she doesn't have the words to alter his definition of her.

ə

there are no longer any real fish. only a flicker of fish – a movement,

the baiting you do talking to me in the street, my back against the
car and you playing the line, hiding behind the tease i rise to, as to
the clover of your smile –

"fish are there to be caught you know."

will i rise? school behaviour a shoal of fish. just as, back then,
swimming through sexual currents looking for eyes as if they
might bridge the gap, flare, romantic semaphore. gone fishing
for compliments recognition is, eyes the lure. allure. not looking
(out) but looking the look for certain eyes, floating around the
places he swam by, i lost myself (as they say) and i did. fall
into invisibility, silvered, dead. i floated up and down the school
yard with the others, eyes reflecting all they saw, blind to myself,

more: hoping to feel that hook when his would connect: "he looked at me!"

all action his, mine merely to be seen. i contend with desire elicited from me. the lure, the bait: i'm worth fishing for.

(how much did he say the boy bragging, how much does a fisherman get per pound on spring salmon now?)

the fishy vocabularies we speak our words through. "the fish never says no," you say, the lure speaking. but watch that fish swim right on by. the fish is after something too. something else.

⁂

imagine her in her element. not to be taken in its restrictive sense as home (is her, closed in).

in her element in other words. blurring the boundary. it's not that she wants to blur difference, to pretend that out is in. already past the gate she's past his point of view as central (hook/lure) to a real she eludes.

free, she multiplies herself in any woman paces the inside of her mind her skin half in half out of the common air she drifts along. casting a thought receives it back, this we of an eye complicit in a smile she gathers fish-quick, taking the measure of their plural depth, she who with every step and never once (-over), desires in the infinitive to utter (outer) her way through: litter. wreckage. salvage of pure intent.

14 / *Rivering*

Ghost

       oily ring shimmering, scintillating round the stern
of the boat you have just painted, *Elma K*, all your ties to shore,
your daughters, wife. Candy cache for the littlest grandchild
peering, short-frocked, over the pen where you below water level
fork up out of the deep – hooked, iced, dressed in slimey
death rendered visible – salmon.

        "Nobody talks about them
anymore," the ghosts that used to rise when you, a child, crossing
the dyke from B.C. Packers, night, saw, Out of the dark this strange
white light, or covering someone's rooftop, invisible to all but
strangers, this blue light telling of death.

 (methane? invisible organic rot? We only know the extinction
of open marsh by concrete, the burial of burial ground by corporate
property.

    But *then* there were places, you say, Chinaman's Hat,
where you couldn't sleep at night, fresh flower in your cabin, for
the host of restless souls' unburied hands outstretcht, returning,
claim their link with the decomposing earth

          (ancestral: fertile as
death: hello briar rose, blackberry & trumpet flower. All their faces
lucent & warmlipt shining before your eyes: teachers, cabaret girls,
longlegged American army wives you chauffeured, cared for, daughters,
friends of your daughters, down thru the water smiles of easy girls,
caught, kore, in the black hole of your eye, yourself a ghost now
of the natural world.

Were you fined? Did you cross the border
inadvertently? Did chart & compass, all direction, fail? Interned,
your people confined to a small space where rebirth, will,
push you out thru rings of material prosperity at war's end
fixed, finally as citizens of an exploited earth: you
drive your own car, construct your own house, create your
registered place at Packers' camp, walk the fine (concrete)
line of private property.

But still at night, tied up in some dark harbour,
it's the cries of women in orgasm you hear echoing with the slap of
water against your hull, coming in, coming in, from far reaches
of the infinite world. And still, at sea, boundaries give way:
white women, white bellies of salmon thieved by powerful boats.

There are no territories. And the ghosts of landlocked camps are
all behind you. Only the blip of depth sounder & fish finder,
harmonic of bells warning a taut line, & the endless hand over
hand flip of the fish into silver pen – successive, infinite –

What do the charts say? Return, return. Return of what doesn't
die. Violence in mute form. Walking a fine line.

Only, always to dream of erotic ghosts of the flowering earth;
to return to a decomposed ground choked by refuse, profit, & the
concrete of private property; to find yourself disinherited from
your claim to the earth.

"Slave of the canneries"

                                          dipping into his album, fisherman's
oldest son. Beached in the mountains. Raised on fish to fish.
As young boatpuller seasick ("my dad, he used to get so
mad at me he'd dump me on the wharf," on solid ground:

Reifel Sanctuary: photos of this man with birds, geese,
tucked under one arm. Working white millionaire's ground
with care, for flood gates, tree growth, observation tower.
Photos of the family house, the family "his" he worked for.
His also, *Lone Eagle*, must go fishing to support, age 23,
nine brothers & sisters & the grandmother whose friend ("she
knew a little bit about such things") delivered them in *this*
house on the drainage canal, company-owned, on pilings so
eaten away they have to jack it with a shingle bolt from
salvaged logs.

                Stench of rotting cannery offal floating by,
shit house seepage from company houses crammed side by side,
footbridges they'd wheel their netcarts over, by ditches drained
by tide. Drainage of this island salvaged out of saltmarsh, these
people drained, resting in their barely salvaged houses where
rats skitter, night, eat at nets drying upstairs the hunger of
eleven people rests on:

                        grace of company loans (debt), of split
cabbage salvaged from slightly wealthier Japanese farms, "our diet
rice, salted fish, & vegetables," day in, day out ("I still like
salted fish"), survival as the *minimum* requirement, nothing more.
hoped for. given the limits (sawmill, farm, or fish ...

                                      Mountains now,
New Denver, rise up round a slow lake windblown sometimes, seeming
to go nowhere. By Carpenter Creek, Orchard so humanly overgrown,

ghetto for evacuees: small shacks again crammed side by side, brown shingled this time fronting the lake. Two thousand Japanese in a few square blocks. Uprooted from the flats, the muddy river, saltwind. Trucked in or brought by train to landlocked winter where the clear air, frozen water's good for TB they say (hemorrhaged in Hastings Park building human pens). "It was a good experience." "How can you say that?" "For the next generation. Look at my daughter, she's a pharmacist!"

    And so strangely pulled out of the delta's restraining ring of debt broken by mass theft (seizure at government level), these impoverished "enemies of the state," transplanted & forced into new growth, shed a mass of memoirs that evidence their real estate the four walls testify to, over the years, room after room added, still not finished.

    To the man who gardens, cares for the old folks' home, caretaker of the ghetto water tower (invisible geese under one arm), marker of past loves & past faces gone with a river cresting, Immoveably settled here like some crustacean in this valley where nothing runs to sea except the water, "one of the few remaining lakes of BC ... sufficiently pure & unpolluted" to drink from / To: the pooled, the still lake, of our muddy & intermingled present.

Winter / rice / tea strain
for Roy Kiyooka

ocha words

– well into winter, we stir up out of what?   what dreams, what cause of communion,   names,   odd stirrings-up of the past as honey pours, *your dream was* this & this reading, this poem pouring this cup of tea proposes (your favourite word)

days stream down any one of the window panes i press my nose against/ you – start & drop the book, your books, all over the floor *so much depends* begin again, pressing these days into pages as if, paged we could pull out any one to savour – this one so young, these

nouns i want to call out to you   winter / rice / tea strain, unlikely sweet tongue, a green hope i bury my face into, steam's slip, & you overheard, breathing yourself into sound

touch

the music rice makes, rice on the tongue in our tea, tea & trout, while outside
rain's quintet batters our ears   hardly the bitterest month, sweet steep, sweet
infusion of green   tipping our lips at the smallest ordinary then crescendo light

through dark your eye

                        stares i stare, in step, the skin of your foot so smooth it
startles, quick

        trout where the darkness lies

                            unformed its leap mere shine
ichthyic, from the base of the spinal column's chorded ascent   (rippling
through the lines of what was planned, unplanned, undone – nothing to
catch our lines haphazard lie

             gen mai cha grain
             between the teeth, still i see

your eye luminant, luminous wonder my eye wanders, amazed & touching
touched with *astony*, love, the thunder of it inflorescent you said a downpour
trout weave through as you described yourself so slow to leap

                                   out in what is

clearly the wonder of budding, leaves, scales of the old
miraculous, adart in the air, as a friend would say, *among*

bachi

sea bush, "small tree" fruit-bearing, salt-sprung   fights your big wood making a world – *poiein* – to its own description,   these drenched leaves straining toward the light, spume, drift of repeated observation drawn to shore

      you offer tea, wipe the wood of the table clearing seawrack, surface grit – we sip to a murmuring of visions, yours, mine, inter-inflected

                                              yet to break our description of the world & thence to see *the dreamer & the dreamed* who's dreaming who? you asked

wind buffets the windowpane   words incessant as rain fall   hear what slips between / this tea we bring to our different lips, this space where nouns unfold

leaf
    by
        leaf

        bits on the floor of the pot we disappear

Here
for David McFadden

is afloat, & cold & moon lights the whole of sky above, lake face below. somewhere a beaver is swimming 60 pounds of oily fur submerged. somewhere fish are skimming the underside of legs & logs, whole auras bristling through water.

are you coming? i call. to whom? two stand on shore, hard-to-see bodies wheeling a single flashlight distance erases, no path across, just flicker writing the dark there where they are.

here i am i cry to the big dipper wheeling so slow overhead no one sees it go by. here i am, osprey cries, black wingspread skimming our heads in dark water. darker logs. white points of stars, *sitareh*, elsewhere flashing into our sky.

we occur in a splash, a rush into black. we occur between this murky bottom & the arched & starred vault of heaven, no camber, no curve or curb now, this chamber roofless floats off into space. heaven is where we occur.

one in the water catches up & we swim to a log that smells of tree skin. imagine beaver allure, living your days in the smell of wet wood, wet fur twisting & diving into the heart of tree remains.

ah, romance, he says. & vivid on the hill, dogs, inchoate, inarticulate, or not in words anyhow, hurl their longing at the moon so full of herself. romance, he says, hit me hard. i wasn't prepared, considering –

a wailing sound, bends round the track in advance of itself, this rival light a late-night freight bewails its coming. in its flare we tread water, watch a rolling roar of white illumine just one side of cottonwoods noon,

afloat on shiny water trying to explain – there weren't many trains on my track. as it fades, as it rolls on into no one's black heaven.

This place full of contradiction
for Betsy Warland

a confusion of times if not of place, though you understood when i said no not the Danish Tearoom – the Indonesian or Indian, was in fact that place of warm walls, a comfortable tarot deck even the lamps pick up your glow, a cabin of going, fjords in there, a clear and pristine look the winds weave through your eyes i'm watching you talk of a different birth, blonde hair on my tongue, of numbers, nine aflush with cappuccino and brandy and rain outside on that street we flash down, laughing with no umbrella, i see your face because i don't see mine equally flush with being, co-incidence being together we meet in these far places we find in each other, it's Sappho i said, on the radio, always we meet original, blind of direction, astonished your hand covers mine walking lowtide strands of Colaba, the lighthouse, Mumbai meaning great mother, you wearing your Irish drover's cap and waiting alive in the glow while i come up worrying Danish and curry, this place full of contradiction – you know, you knew, it was the one place i meant.

Prairie
for Betsy

in this land the rivers carve furrows and canyons as sudden to the eye as if earth opened up its miles and miles of rolling range, highway running to its evercoming horizon, days of it, light picking flowers. your blackeyed susans are here, my coral weed in brilliant patches, and always that grass frayed feathery by the season, late, and wild Canada geese in the last field. i imagine your blue eye gathering these as we go, only you are not here and the parched flat opens up: badlands and hoodoos, that river with dangerous currents you cannot swim, TREACHEROUS BANK, sandstone caving in: and there she goes, Persephone caught in a whirlwind the underside churns up, the otherwise of where we are, cruising earth's surface, gazing on it, grazing like those 70 million year old dinosaurs, the whole herd browsing the shore of Bearpaw Sea which ran all the way in up here, like Florida, she said, come in from the desert region hungry for grass (or flowers) when something like a flashflood caught them, their bones all these years later, laid out in a whirlpool formation i cannot see (that as the metaphor) up there on the farthest hoodoo, those bright colours she keeps stressing, the guy in the red shirt, metal flashing, is not Hades but only the latest technician in a long line of measurers. and earth? i have seen her open up to let love in, let loose a flood, and fold again, so that even my fingers could not find their way through all that bush, all that common day rolling unbroken.

Kore
for Betsy

    no one wears yellow like you, excessive and radiant storehouse of sun, skin smooth as fruit but thin, leaking light. (i am climbing toward you out of the hidden.) no one shines like you, so that even your lashes flicker light, amber over blue (*amba*, amorous Demeter, you with the fire in your hand, i am coming to you). no one my tongue burrows in, whose wild flesh opens wet, tongue seeks its nest, amative and nurturing (here i am you) lips work towards undoing (*dhei*, female, sucking and suckling, fecund) spurt / spirit opening in the dark of earth, *yu!* cry jubilant excess, your fruiting body bloom we issue into the light of, sweet, successive flesh …

"Two women in a birth"

what is there between them? in this *in*. desire in their desire room in their room somebody in the body of not in but in the doubling of. mise en abyme. out in the outback we are in the desert then or the abandoned. *desert of ice of love of stolen dreams desert of the heart.* but what if the boundary goes walking? refuses to be that place the hero enters with his *gold* his *drums* his *caravans* – o *the desert generals the desert fathers the desert rats the desert revolution.* (we saw hoofprints of camels and never camels but scrub and many varieties of: we stood in the middle of nothing and it was full. bleak obstacle-boundary-space to and for his adventures, ground to his figure and exploits, grave-cave she has rolled over in all that red dust (the year is endless here) given herself a shake and birthed into subject. the inconceivable doubling herself into life no slouch-backed beast (even double humped) heading for Bethlehem but the doubling of 'woman' into hundreds camped in the middle of desert outside Pine Gap's nuclear base, and the voice of the desert is the sound of their singing out their anger relentless and slow as dunes walking. we are off the train in order to be in the desert no longer the object of exchange but she-and-she-who-is-singing (as the women have always sung) this body *my (d)welling place*, unearthed.

"Imagin-a-nation in the heart of"

as the heart surrounded by all this flesh feels its weight (the pressure of pumping blood through such a system) throws up its hands in surrender the heart is never isolate never away (women cannot get away) as the people who inhabit this emptiness will tell you heartland laid waste (desert is not waste) dug up for uranium irradiated in nuclear testing (the fragile ecosystem the heart is) will fence off sacred sites to keep out the acquisitive heart is consumed the heart is not allowed to throb for pleasure in what surrounds (imagine a nation at home in the "deathless body") the heart must be used (up) (imagine a nation uncommitted to surplus profit) working for love not pay imagination is at home with emptiness imagination a-muses herself with the emptiness of words and boards the train of the sentence empty-handed and makes off with it de-riding the end point of the Final Product (she is not for termination after all) she is well on her way to de-railing the "long straight" which can only see its own track while she is out on either side (surrounded she knows does not mean surrender) she is also she is desert come in waves the waves she rides she rises up and overflows the words a round around the word *surround*

There is a door

> *... other than that which opens to the known world*

drawn in the steamed-up windows of the house a house (windows and mouth, lopsided plume) that bares opaque aspects of the soul (no kidding) the way words exit her place of abode, steamed up, where is she anyhow? keeping house as if keeping herself meant hugging a shadowy wall she is playing house without the means with all the right words (keeping it nice) and somehow still feels left outside

he has a full house, three of a kind and a pair no repairing to where she hears he is scaling walls, floodlit –

the depression of solitaire: fear of claws in the legal because (she is tied up inside it all) believing what they said, that she would die if she went through that door …

where women meet together where the words face up, are heard – i know what you mean – in these small houses walls are falling

while his back meeting rain on the street slickers into the Buccaneer, relief, the reign of conversation here behind glass fogged up and closed in, it's in-house news exchanged with change or beer the currency of who makes it here

playing to a small house, house of the ascendant, house of commons, stars parading through their phrases, stars or tiny lights –

that there's only so much power, not enough to go round, to light up windows on the outside of town / the known

the indifferent news

we are giving up on, moving out of solitaire into a clearer sense of what relates us: this solar river this windy oikos simultaneous her sisterfire at the mouth at the mouth borne inside each of us saying what women see is flooding out the old inside / outside of our minds

Shrimping

stark against the green bushes green water lucent salmon net, these
steamsprayed with tar caught up at the boom and flowing like a
dirge

dirige Domine who hath dominion dominate in techne lord of the
nets

their boats lined up and wearing shrouds of black for the dark of
bottom waters shrimp who do not pray crawl

diminutive and
shrinking, wrinkled akin to cabbage with crumpled leaves acurl
where babies, baby shrimp he said look at them curled in their cans
just waiting to be picked, *crevette*, little shrimp, sitting on his fingers
stuck up playfully there and there my sweet looking good enough
to eat she was wearing her short dress with frilly underwear, so pink
this little crack crevasse (la la) we have taken over this fissure in
the gender of it all

this fiction pink for little girls that we were
the ones plying the net, fore-ply alive in the reddening of desire
from the raw to the cooked dressing her feminine with just a bit of
sauce, you don't want to look like a boy do you? widening the gap
(crevasse) a finger's width just letting her know what's him fishing
for her below

and the net goes roaring with the lead weight of it dead weight down
to unseen dark her body crawls feathery legs (undrowned) feathery
head light barely makes out the splurr and creep of net in the tone of his
words my little shrimp

the name of the net   the name of the net   the name of the net
later she cannot dredge it up at all

from *Mauve*
for Nicole Brossard

skin and its evidents

to think   to write
sometimes resembles in
undecidable features

fiction culture cortex

M A U V E

M A U V E

cortex fiction culture

stains the other
mew   maiwa   mauve
malva rose core text
fiction rings round
skin immersed in
resemblance takes
the stain, sense
roseblue in tissue re-
membering

Small print
for Betsy

i

how little the reach, what is *love* love? its
impossible repeat attenuated through telephone
wire the light letter language of "fax it," hearts
darling and x's intend body's imprint, stand in
for the unremitting smell of your skin just there at
neck's bony hollow in your hair both kinds that
arc the pelvic ridge keys your other speech
close up and swollen lips aflare with wet
declaration *bold face* – without which i sleep
small print in the white of the page

iii

reading your voice attentive to solitude a
transient space love infiltrates anticipates
the feel of your skin its smell no word (nearness
then) resplendent breasting under the covers a
breathing space the city occludes its neon news
your voice removed my body walks its carbon
copy of yours deep in the bone

v

to reach those little loves the pain of hills
animal words love-stark, enter in white a
void of cross-hatching covering distance unknown
intent scrawls xmas drift along the creek i follow
your declarative slant as you ascend out of the
limits of love a joy you wished language written
in quick gesture bold stride new reference i
try to decipher

Booking passage

> *You know the place: then*
> *Leave Crete and come to us*
>   Sappho / Mary Barnard

this coming & going in the dark of early morning, snow scribbling its thaw line round the house. we are undercover, under a cover of white you unlock your door on this slipperiness.

to throw it off, this cover, this blank that halts a kiss on the open road. i kiss you anyway, & feel you veer toward me, red tail lights aflare at certain patches, certain turns my tongue takes, provocative.

we haven't even begun to write … sliding the in-between as the ferry slips its shoreline, barely noticeable at first, a gathering beat of engines in reverse, the shudder of the turn to make that long passage out –

the price paid for this.

we stood on the road in the dark. you closed the door so carlight wouldn't shine on us. our kiss reflected in snow, the name for this.

under the covers, morning, you take my scent, writing me into your cells' history. deep in our sentencing, i smell you home.

there is the passage. there is the booking – & our fear of this.

you, sliding past the seals inert on a log boom. you slide & they don't raise their heads. you are into our current now of going, not inert, not even gone as i lick you loose. there is a light beginning over the ridge of my closed eyes.

passage booked. i see you by the window shore slips by, you reading Venice our history is, that sinking feel, those footings under water. i nose the book aside & pull you forward gently with my lips.

a path, channel or duct. a corridor. a book & not a book. not booked but off the record. this,

irresistible melt of hot flesh. fur line & thaw line align your long wet descent.

nothing in the book says where we might head. my tongue in you, your body cresting now around, around this tip's lick suck   surge rush of your coming in other words.

we haven't even begun to write ... what keeps us going, this rush of wingspread, this under (nosing in), this wine-dark blood flower. this rubbing between the word and our skin.

❧

"tell me, tell me where you are" when the bush closes in, all heat a luxuriance of earth so heavy i can't breathe the stifling wall of prickly rose, skreek of mosquito poised ... for the wall to break /

                the wall that isolates, that i so late to this: it doesn't, it slides apart – footings, walls, galleries, this island architecture

one layer under the other, memory a ghost, a guide, histolytic where the pain is stored, murmur, mer-*mère*, historicity stored in tissue, text ... a small boat, fraught, trying to cross distance, trying to find that passage (secret) in libraries where whole texts, whole persons have been secreted away.

original sin he said was a late overlay. & under that, & under that? sweat pouring down, rivers of thyme & tuberose in the words that climb toward your scanning eyes

> *She shouts aloud, Come! we know it;*
> *thousand-eared night repeats that cry*
> *across the sea shining between us*

🙠

this tracking back & forth across the white, this tearing of papyrus crosswise, this tearing of love in our mouths to leave our mark in the midst of rumour, coming out.

… to write in lesbian.

the dark swell of a sea that separates & beats against our joined feet, islands me in the night, fear & rage the isolate talking in my head. to combat this slipping away, of me, of you, the steps … what was it we held in trust, tiny as a Venetian bead, fragile as words encrusted with pearl, *mathetriai*, not-mother, hidden mentor, lost link?

to feel our age we stood in the road in the dark, we stood in the roads & it was this old, a ripple of water against the hull, a coming & going

we began with …

her drowned thyme & clover, fields of it heavy with dew our feet soak up, illicit hands cupped one in the other as car lights pick us out. the yell a salute. marked, we are elsewhere, translated here ...

like her, precisely on this page, this mark: *a thin flame runs under / my skin.* twenty-five hundred years ago, this trembling then. actual as that which wets our skin her words come down to us, a rush, poured through the blood, this coming & going among islands is.

In the current

>   ... *one discovers the immense landscape ... of the passage.*
>   Hélène Cixous

    isle isolé,
        pain enislanded,
            i stand at your door quick with your here, my coming pleasure on the rein leaps with anticipation, pleasure & grief so wound together

It is the passage that can appear ...

with anticipation of your opening, your light step to the door a landscape that unfolds its coastal curves, its rocks non-negotiable, its sudden isthmus isthmus oh hello
        is most fragile for the mouth that connects

        ... most difficult.

i'm island, o stranded isolate that hesitates once more at a singular mountain (omitting mountains' joint footing underwater, o joined *jouissant*, the world is round she sang)

at your door the body in its forward motion trembles, trans-lated, is (o *les volées*

your door – you open it, light flares in a great wedge from beyond your shoulders

    It happens in a flash. In a leap. Without transition ...

welcome streaming out of your eyes. & risk. all the bodies we have loved
pass their shadows in transit between us

                                              on the buoyant, in the current
of a passage impossible & yes, in trust.

Generation, generations at the mouth

clans of salmon, Chinook, coho gathering just off shore, backbones no longer intact, steam-pressured in millions of cans, picked clean barbecue leavings in a thousand garbage bags ripped open by cats, rats, they can't find their way back

what is the body's blueprint?

return what is solid to water, the first people said
returned, every bone intact
generates the giving back of race, kind, kin

choked in urban outfalls, fished as they aim for rivers sediment-thick with runoff, *tamahnous* of the wild they hover, sonar streaks, impossible vision-glitches, outside pens where farmed look-alikes grow pale & drugged

kin, wild skin, wild & electric at the mouth where rivers disappear in the that that is not that, the chinook can't find their way back

come out of the blue: this flow, these energy rivers & wheels, radiant giving unlocked. & not this frozen, this canned product eagles once stripped, eagles, bears, going, gone, hungry & wild outside shut doors where light pools & we pore over stock market news, refuse, refuse our interrelation, refuse to pour back

what *is* the body's blueprint? impermanent, shifting energy blocks in its own becoming, a stream & streaming out to the void where rivers lose themselves in the bardo as many beings as waves gather at any opening, those in-between and not-yet ones that race a river of sperm to be here now, light pour, each cell in its dying turn returns

what is the mouth of the river now? a toxic 0 of emptiness? teeming hole of ever-becoming we create? re-entry. re-turn. verbing the noun out of its stuck edges and into occurrence, currents, *curre-* . . . we've lost the verb in our currency a frozen exchange streaming emptiness

                        (they're fishing in London now)

at the mouth of the river, clans of the possible are gathering, the chinook, the coho rivering just offshore are us.

"Complicated"

       "we make ourselves complicated"
       Rinpoche in the *gompa*
       yellow sail / swallowtail
       large as a laugh
       attaches itself to his sleeve

sitting simply "this
human body" vivid &
"at last attained"
      (fuchsia perfect
fragile & changing
with each breath

      (large as a laugh
      & flutter-brief

wind-, lake-, pine-
mothers all round
tsombus, devas, pretas
all breath-beings & non-breath sky

offered thus

Years Ago (from *The Gull*, Act I)

KURI
(sung poem, rhythm not matched with drum beats)

JI: years ago, a bride she came across the sea
leaving the boats of Mio, her parents' temple home
leaving a prayer at the Dragon-God Shrine
at Kobe she said goodbye

SASHI
(recitation, sung)

WAKI: passing Cape Hinomisaki

JI: with wet sleeves
she turned from the headland she knew,
gazing instead at the promise
held in her hand,
a small photo of her husband-to-be

WAKI: young, firm of body

JI: and the words he sent
a river teeming with fish, at its mouth
a village newly-built, wide-open sky —

WAKI: a future for her shining there

SHITE *(in Japanese)*: I saw my future shining just ahead

SHITE slips off cloak and rises.

JI: she saw her future shining there

KUSE
(core narrative, song matched with drum beats accompanied by dance)

SHITE stands on bridgeway, raising sleeve-wings, moves onstage and begins to dance slowly, then speeds up after she sings her single line below.

JI: only a dream as things turned out
      he was older than his photo, and the place itself
      a wild estuary the winter winds keened through
      thin walls of TB huts,
      the strikes, the babies,

      debt an endless round he pulled us from
      to own his boat, his net, his home at last

Uchikiri as Shite dances.

      but there were taunts and threats
      and then the war –
      they took our boats, our homes
      our cars we'd worked so hard for
      – all lost, seized and sold
      to pay for our keep as "enemy
      aliens" – condemned,

      families split and sent
      from the coast to camps faraway,
      in icy crowded huts and ghost
      town rooms we were penned up
      in the frozen mountains.

44 / *Rivering*

SHITE *(in Japanese)*:
          fury scalds my wings remembering

JI: how gulled we were, her cry
            her splash in the spray of China Hat's
            seething storm –

During the following, SHITE moves to bridgeway, turns to face standing WAKI and WAKITSURE, swoops towards them, turns again, and moves down bridgeway.

JI: strange, her story resembles our mother's
            – wait, he calls, who are you?
            as she lifts drenched wings torn
            ragged in the round of migration
            only a gull's shriek beats the air –
            fool Mio-birds,

            go home! go home!

On the last line SHITE raises a "wing." Brief and piercing Nôkan flute solo as SHITE exits rapidly.

JI: mirage of the wind, rain fury,
            no woman after all, but a gull, a gull
            – yet she did speak.

Singing grass

> *Sais-tu toujours les mots transcrits*
> *Hors de nos murs?*
> Sveva Caetani

singing grass – goes still when she tiptoes near –

she squats. hands, probing carefully, part the dry rustle-grasses back on themselves, on dusty sage –

and there it jumps quick sticklike click, grey elbow jut-outs unfold – wings, oh, bright halo afloat on desert air, *farfalla!*

cicada, her father says, that's what people call it here – *non è farfalla, mia figlia* – sikayda. her father knows everything, insects and fruit trees, different languages, desert turning into *paradiso*.

sì sì

    che? (oh)

        kay da

the lonesome wail of a train sounds somewhere beyond them through the hills of this parched Okanagan land. her father is growing an orchard with his Italian hands, with his bare hands. fresh water and dust, their new leaf, leaves, blossoming. and look, Sveva, there go our

secret horses, horses of the imagination, running between the rows. he
points them out to her and laughs at her squint in the heat haze.

> *Re*
> how does a painter grow?

she remembers stone walls, archways, bell tower, her father a duke
and a prince back in Sermoneta, in Teano. but that doesn't matter,
he says, because here we are just people among people. true, we have
an unbroken line of nobility behind us but it is up to us to sustain
what truly matters in this life.

la linea / Papa Leone / life line
running through the valley bottom
her mother Ofelia traces
the lightest of touch
on her hand

no, no. the soul's journey, he tells her, down its *wonder-river*, through
canyons of impasse, through dead citadels, dead seasons of fate,

wonder as integral to him as the pulsing of his blood.

iron line / lead pencil
leads, and she is following

leaning up against him, feeling the warmth of his arm as he reads out a passage from the book his finger marks for her. smiling up at the lean nose she loves, the steady eyes that hold her in hope as he holds a line from Dante in memory. her Papa, *for whom remote lands and seeming barrenness promised mystery and adventure*. for whom the horses of the imagination roam and run, *rush like rain*.

Recap

through paint and graphite
child eye trained by a Russian
artist, trips back to Europe
Ofelia's compensation for
uprooting from Rome

human, anguished and inexpressibly lonely

boxcar wail of away, invitation and link to fountains and cathedral bell-towers, *la alta moda*, villas of the Caetanis, the Fabianis, *il teatro*, fabulous architecture once their immediate here. now the canyon their train passes through is without habitation – perhaps a lone squatter, an abandoned prospector's shack –

Solo fantasma.

You remember

you remember – what is it you remember?

the feel of home, that moment of coming into your body, its familiar ache and shift, its little cough of consciousness resuming (Monday claims). i'm awake. i can't quite see your face assume its usual definition. your shoulder rises like a hill i climb getting out on my side of the bed to pad to the sunroom, lift the blind on a spectral world. one early dog racing across the park, its breath steaming up through pallid light, though it isn't light, not yet. still in bed, you turn to rise like some revenant, asking what time is it?

in the still of the day we bring something to burn. the smells of home, not roasted barley flour but tea, tea and toast. these small ceremonies ribbon through the days we share. and share, continuous, with what is gone.

it was July, that radiant kind of morning when all of outside shines in, calling the body out to play, light pristine, re-arisen, chickadee's two-note shrill euphoric, *here / i'm here* – this *joyant* pouring in with sun across a kitchen nook amist with memory smoke, his breakfast cigarette, my usual struggle with a five year-old, eat your cereal, you can't go out until you eat. while all three of us know, between sips of this and that, only two blocks away the waves are lapping tenderly at sand, at soon-to-be bare feet, a thrill of seaweed under the gulls' dip and shriek.

how it was, that morning of liquid flight when my father's call came: i can't wake her up, his voice like a child's, crushed, lost. i've tried, she won't wake up.

and birds, in the corner of an eye as i stared unfocussed at their sky-writing: flap flap, soar. their sanskrit.

why does the eye slide off? the mind refuse anything more than grabbing at keys, making quick arrangements, then tearing through the parkway across the bridge along the Upper Levels, thinking glorious glorious morning, everyone driving their usual cavalcade of must-do's and if only's, thinking how can this be? this sudden gap.

gape. a wound that is love and not love.

you can't do that, she told me over the phone when we'd come back to the city and i wanted to paint what would be the baby's room. you can't paint when you're pregnant. that limiting fear i bridled at. it's latex, mom. we painted together in a memory loop from my childhood, water instead of turps, a splotch of robin's egg blue on the soft sag of her cheek, her perfection at cleaning brushes. paint moons at the roots of our nails, and her latest conspiracy theory about her doctor, her dentist.

A pleasant glow of sentiment was shed by a light rosily shaded and suffused.

that too. its pleated shade, its fluted glass stem a little tippy, casting a glow to read by. a satin quilt pulled up to her chin, hands holding the well-used public library smell of plastic covering a queen's unbent head, the bloody intrigue of courtiers and kings, while all the while steam rose from the rose-patterned teacup beside her, twisted and thinned to nothing in the pinkpearl glow.

rapid overlay, one place-time on another, as if we're actually in the movement between, memory cascading its lightdrenched moments and then suddenly that single jet of recognition, parallel perhaps, that allows us to see, paradoxically, this place we're in the midst of . . .

incredible. conflicting with explanation.

underlay, as if
her body under the
lay of the city under
lies it

to feel at home in just that particular light before haze moves in – moments only – brightens Spode blue mountains dusted white today. Crown leaning its dazzle over the blue shoulder of Grouse. against their steady presence the restless filigree of leafless birch. waver, tremble. still getting used to this particular sense of history as missed story, shadowing place.

Walking

walking out, walking our solid and intimate bodies down neighbouring streets lesbian-friendly or not, noting the houses other dykes enter, the rooms of artists of one stripe or another. taking note of averted faces, elderly shoppers, ferocious dealers and those strung-out. or those who nod and smile hello. walking our passing bodies down streets of layered lives, lapidary, set in cement. the remains of stories.

touching the tree
touching the fence
alley alley home ...

or moments like that warm expanse of shallow ocean coming in, body of water rippling sandflat history in names (Malaspina, Narváez). cool up to our knees, the dog cavorting free of heat stupor (*Sutil*, *Mexicana* and *Discovery*). fur sprinkles glisten. late light's almost amber, *super-natural*, islands to the west mere silhouettes (Valdéz, Galiano, all that's left of their encounter with Vancouver some two centuries ago and just offshore – the same and not the same river-ocean then).

we cavort, wade, turn to go – and there, hallucinatory, banked in ahistorical distance, a vertical construct of glass and concrete flares its dazzle, flashes *"world-class city,"* the city Vancouver *did not know that there would one day be*....

Tree-song (from *Shadow Catch*, Act I)

TREE SPIRIT
& JI:
: Between these interlaced and
whispering leaves,
hand talk with wind, outstretched and
offering inter-speak
with passing cloud and rain for
generations generous.

TREE SPIRIT:
: Hear cautious feet
deer shuffle in
shadows, a knock-
knock-knock, no
flicker thinks it's *his*
ridged bark that
tree-frog climbs —

TREE SPIRIT
& JI:
: The rise and fall of song's
wash ever-tidal wave
so intertempo'd here.

Tree Spirit moves towards Waki and bends over him.

TREE SPIRIT:
: Can you hear?
from your separate hell
can you hear my hello?

She sweeps one hand over the sleeping boy's body with no response from him.

TREE SPIRIT: We'll leaf-talk then.

TREE SPIRIT   Moon-sap-rain
& JI: relations untold, unnamed,
                   'til human tellers gave
                   their word to us,
                   K'emk'émelay'

TREE SPIRIT: Here we stood,
                    here we flourished,

TREE SPIRIT   Windstrung, sung,
& JI: let go, re-flourished
                   countless green hellos
                   in the inter-species song,
                   this rhythm ground.

"Spectacular"

                CPR's new Pier, gangway descent, water lap at
buildings's back, open harbour. Turret front, its portico wide
sweep of waiting room, Custom's sticky city entry: Pier D
long-timbered wharf that thousands walk

                                          in time, Seabirds
trawling wind.

            Incessant, shipping

        several transcontinental trains daily
        white *Empresses* from the Orient calling

passenger disembarcation, for, he remarked with pride, the
coming metropolis.   High-buttoned boots a stamp of
civility. Lions chasmic yawning. Royalty on a cowcatcher
view the Rockies. O Empire's furthest outpost cradled
by inland sea the ships go down to. And they crowd
around   as so many shadows view the new arrivals

Gateway to ... capitalize (on) a labour pool, their East our
western sun, sets a time of *terrific coolie movements . . . The
Chinese were going through Canada in transit and were
heavily guarded*   THIS WAY (only)

                          Unseen from the first
reverse:
               'Back home' THAT way: lace, pianos, lamps, all
tinkly equipage, by royal steamer

                              (*Celestials* pig-tail
tied, shipped to Victoria, no siree, *no Chinee loggers in the
Brighouse claim*)

                    "At-home" refugees from rain
chatter of opera house   blue willow ware   *The Geisha*
that "infernal houseboy"   standing near

                                      tea and silk

first thing off the ship and onto the train east ... silk train....
heavily insured

                    against time or accident or loss (whose?

a virtual holocaust,

                          unreal they said   of *Flames traveling*
underneath the dock ... mock civility rules o citizen ... *at a*
terrific pace, Fireman Bird had *difficulty getting down the*
Granville Street hill ...

                    so thick   was it

with viewers,   inferno-drawn.

To navigate

                      grey-green fathoms, un/ fathomed
intent, a word to be applied only eye-desire,
hands, hips, lift, body parts in sync, incline (rise)
to join ... what am i then, air? (tug, that makes a
bridge rise, by which, bewitched, i feel your thrust,
my lift, want

                    not sky, that inch by inch
straining upward intent ...

            Bridge circuit snapped, red
light flashing,   heads into autonomous
alien ...
        sky /gap / electrical ab-
                  sense air is,

how it parts, struck by down-descending
 weight to hold (just for a

    Second

        Narrows, as it was

once, coming down. Tide swirls under long gone
bridge lumbering flat now, trains roll on

low bascule (buttocks), suck of tide requiring greater
clearance for this inlet's "bridge of sighs," two freighters
hit, then *Pacific Gatherer* knocks out its span. Erect
deck, jackknifes to sky

            gap, a break

in the crossing, tide swirl to green, still green North Shore
rail lines and traffic propose, despite Depression, vertical
lift span that will (will it?) clear shipping. Red light flashing
NO   farther ...   watch that span shudder into sky above
steep bore wave, the tide

                                  that swallows men.

Third try crossing, new high-level cantilever reach, out to
... (air) ...

                      jumble of twisted truss span steel
workers flung from / to, murky tide divers lift bodies from.

Now at night, near *Chay-chil-wuk, near or narrow,* lost
ironworkers ghost on through   intent   on

the join)

Comes walking

                up through horror in the way of
vision, salt

         sh'te she'd come through walking
wood block paving cedar cracked dark wit she'll come
heron eye and quick

              kelp feather hair her stilted walk

come squawking grief transformed

through storm drain city outfall metaphor she wades
through rain's choleric traffic thrum he slows

        :that bristle shudder hers (feathers long
along her neck) and peering back intuits   disregards...

is gone

twice shafted (*slime fisher*) diacetyl bitter bittern

           body as gift spurned grawk

Marine ah

                    body of water you came wet you
come reaches of the sea through metropolis mother tide
docked and watermark culture your first growth log
saloon hotel boots you sideslip keels

                                    to dwell in
habit streets you lap you shine rain's anterior headturner
albedo gleam unfurled

                small arm of the sea
                            fringed

infringed by dockside gantry cranes Beacon K-line rolling
stock she current *with spirit or energy a lot more than objects*
mirrors dazzle creek wise or riverine with its tip to art deco
sign Rainier's *all-woman character* once restaurant-bar its
taxi stand for 1920s black maria lineup long skirt straw
hat thought of entrance later 40s girl shoeshine smile to
his pervasive business shoe his

                              liquid lunch in the ell
bo hail below she fur b'lows in cars later incurs hardly a
culture of safety   these liquid assets about to drain

        the real

estate cult she streams through outfall tidal muck harbour
rain striated heart 'n all its submerged relations mourning

what can't be replaced   the rift   the mind   cracks in the
carefully patterned concrete

                        still Muriel mar a sign
the rain's a *place where hope comes* mildewed maybe
rusted fire escape impossible routes gnarl up through
grime to white full shine in her

                          elle ll a live oh

Through cloud

                      white shock blue Grouse willowware
shades glaze those two facing Sisters hyas muckamuck
renamed couchant imperial untracked Crown looms legalized
so close down Main tonight hope snows veins eyes loose
change names liquid

              drip eaves long gone in re-
build demolished reconstructed viz city market dream the
locals by early water under bridge no willow sole perch
sturgeon at False Creek points slaughterhouse then sawmill
muck
       mark it
            a market econ oh

who managing whose house it runs down to

                              e-merge

a metro built on labour's back on brick or wood slats glitz
'n bling now wallow in stock collapse concrete drips snow
line no-show line down blue shopping or shipping out all
water under the bridge

                  capitalized on

Suezmax tanker traffic liquid asset runoff
liquid(i)city
       's melt oolichan near gone

it's warming up
        so grab a

rainhat eh once cedar see reigning oil's long
reach it rains for free
        still
            it rains

Lift. step. drop

                    this never-ending speak its inner hook some flash cognition continuity leap onto the next   crosscut any sidestreet offers rhyme a glance   solid   chairleg stays   carpet hot under sock by gas fire's 1920 rose   a rise once out of American eyes no fumble that neo-rosary a hooker   all toes   slow unfold incessant seesaw glitch then shift on left   why toes rolling stretch slow moment um momentum meaning oh that catch… not so close scarlet calves in perfect sync say   a pass a handout Rose rose the story goes   old ever-saw once seen   withdraws ground the heel ·slow
                           lift & wait to let
                                          (it)   go

Afterword: Immediacies of Writing

so the moon was painting in radium real this unreal-ing of
foreground/background where she leans a luminous imprint
paper remembers her, arms brushed with white pear's fishy
scent ... "an old one that, if it could talk would tell you
many things." transplant, she took her stand, in drift, in
a river of grass flowing over her walk   immersion as
complete as the pouring of water into water

                                                        this is not
background.

From "Reading it" in *Salvage* (1991), one of the poems later devised from *Steveston* discards. This particular passage describes and quotes the elderly wife of an Issei shipwright and fisherman living in Steveston. Sometimes, unknowingly, one writes a few lines that continue to reverberate as some kind of pointer for future years of writing.

  Perhaps because I began writing in short lines, prose whether in long lines or in a prose poem opened as an arena of transgression for me. Prose felt ongoing, ecstatic in its potential for syntactic permutation, its rhythmic runs and sudden verbal associations, while poetry felt more measured, contained, committed to the versus, that break and semantic slide back to the left margin.

  As a young poet in the early 1960s, I inherited discussions about free verse from the Modernist poets and their experimentations with prose. From the ecstasies of Whitman, or Saint-John Perse, or Rimbaud, I moved with greater need to the sinuous sentences of Virginia Woolf, Djuna Barnes, Gertrude Stein. As a woman, especially a woman poet, the need to transgress limits of gender, class, and inherited culture seemed more possible in the relatively open space of prose, but a prose that could meet poetry in its attentiveness to language. After all, I had also inherited from the New American poets and their sources attention to the rhythms and diction of contemporary speech. So here, at the beginning of my writing, was a basic dualism between my woman's body and then-inherited place in the world, and a male-engendered poetic and grasp of that world.

In prose there is the appeal of the rhythmic run of a sentence, the way a thought will grow, extending itself through rhythmic variation, syntactic possibility, and melodic association to branch out into extended meaning – as if a sentence might embrace the multiplicities of an immediate world/whatever is local to it. This movement from word to world suggests a real that depends on the often unstated I behind those words, whoever is speaking/singing/uttering (outering) her way into meaning others might recognize. The hope for communication, communication as both common in the sense of shared and a making known of individual perception.

My emergence as a poet coincided with large-scale political awakenings: the civil rights, anti-war, feminist, and later post-colonial and lesbian/gay-rights movements of two decades, the 1960s through the 1980s. In the early 60s, mentors such as Charles Olson, Robert Duncan, and Robert Creeley attuned my awareness to such awakenings. I began to listen to voices and their diction, markers of social class, gender, ethnic background, political stance, or religious affiliation. This led to early work in aural (or oral, but I like that insistence on listening in aural) history and, subsequently, a certain amount of intertextuality in my poetry.

However, poetry has never been for me simply a form of reportage. Composition, the act of putting words together, is full of immediacies. There is always edge, the edge a poem rides in its coming into form out of the inchoate, the formless.

Any writer is familiar with wordlessness – or let's say perhaps the phenomenon of wording, the astonishment of a word or phrase rising to meet the page "live" in its connection with a previous word or phrase, this against that empty prior-to-wording state that can be a sort of patient fishing before anything recognizable surfaces as "catch." And the "catch" is slippery, comes in a backwards–forwards motion suggesting new variations of thought as it refers back to earlier ones. A word in its immediate claim on attention will relate as much as it also isolates, based, as words are, on small and very specific distinctions (that "l" for instance that separates *world* from *word*) and their capacity for play – add *elle* to word and you get a world of difference.

At the most immediate level in composition (crossing a threshold with each word or phrase, sometimes each syllable, certainly each line), words come shadowed by their histories, half-forgotten remnants of past language activity, just as particular people and sites come shadowed by their stories of past actions and relations. Poems often begin for me as a moment's thought-activity gathering at the threshold of larger unworded potential ...

– "You're very beautiful," her words interrupt, float up from the deck below. In that moment I hear the insistent coo-cOO-roo of a collared-dove that has been haunting our neighbourhood and now announces its presence on the birch behind my window,

… potential as large as what IS this life we are caught up in together? This groundless limitless web of relations multi-dimensional, folding and unfolding in drift, each of us small knots of radiating (and potentially radiant) connection on which we project fixed identity, transient as we are, constantly changing, becoming and breaking. How can a poem, that small immediate web of words, point at or gesture towards some of this largeness?

In its coming into words (the immediate act of composition), a poem will generate a current, a charge as it develops. This current pulls into it material that may simply be flotsam (surface float) or may further the current, twist and merge with it. Writing – not the fingers on the keyboard or the pencil (yes, their rhythms and movements too) so much as listening, listening in the echo chamber language operates in charged thinking. Hearing other / alter(ering) even errant possibilities of connection on both phonemic and semantic levels, on memory levels (resonating phrases from others' work through time), all points of contact in the resonating web of language that is our medium for thought.

Although I've written poems based on visits elsewhere, I find it difficult to write anything but notes, journal entries while travelling. So I write at home in all that surrounds the act of writing at any point: house, neighbourhood, city, larger coastal terrain, each with its diverse inhabitants – widening and interconnected spheres of immediacies experienced within personal, collective, and historical webs of relationship. The linear depth of the historical, the lateral sweep of the surround. Within these, connection and continuity, the basis for narrative – but also the increasing breakages our info-addicted globalized late-capitalist culture inflicts on wordless environments. In this current (warming) climate we get news stories that move attention rapidly from crisis to crisis without follow-through or adequate investigation of causes. We get people torn from their localities and community stories that tell them who they are. Instead, we get virtual realities that entertain, entail illusory images of who we might become, putting us out of touch, out of actual contact with the physical context on/in which humans exist interdependently with so many other forms of life. The give-and-take of those myriad connections in the ecological web of which we are a part – how they fade out as mere background

Afterword / 65

noise. To write against this is to respond to background. To listen in, give close attention to almost inaudible connections even as they transform and change. The web of language is its own web, but in its multiplicities it parallels those other myriad connections in which we also live.

 There is a particular connection that has given life to this book, a connection to be honoured, namely Susan Knutson's dedication to the project of editing this selected poetry. Despite being the victim of a head-on highway collision in September 2012, despite subsequent surgeries, constant pain, and learning to walk again, she has persisted in reading, selecting, and corresponding with me across the distance between hospitals in Halifax, then her home in Weymouth, and my home in Vancouver. From the miracle of her survival to this book: a long journey, the result of heroic effort on her part. All my gratitude to you, Susan.

– Daphne Marlatt

Acknowledgements

Daphne Marlatt and Susan Knutson thank Brian Henderson and Neil Besner for supporting this project from the beginning, and we join with them and the fine team at WLUP in thanking Betsy Warland and Nicole Brossard for their generous collaboration. For permission to republish works still in print we gratefully acknowledge Talonbooks (*The Gull, This Tremor Love Is,* and *Liquidities*), Ronsdale Press (*Steveston*), and Random House (*The Given*).

"Street opera" and "Coming in, who," from the sequence "Month of Hungry Ghosts," were published in *The Capilano Review* 16–17 (1979) and collected in *Ghost works* (Edmonton: NeWest Publishers, 1993).

"June near the river Clyst, Clust, clear. Clystmois this holding wet & clear," "Combe Martin, house martin, Martinmas, Saint Martin, martial swords & plowshares," and "Avebury awi-spek, winged from buried (egg," were published in *How Hug a Stone* (Winnipeg: Turnstone Press, 1983) and collected in *Ghost works* (NeWest Publishers, 1993).

"Litter. wreckage. salvage" was published in *Salvage* (Red Deer: Red Deer College Press, 1991).

"Ghost" and "'Slave of the canneries'" were published in *Steveston*, with photographs by Robert Minden (3rd ed. Vancouver: Ronsdale Press, 2001; 2nd ed. Edmonton: Longspoon Press, 1984; 1st ed. Vancouver: Talonbooks, 1974).

"Winter/ rice / tea strain" was published as a limited-edition chapbook (British Columbia: (m)Other Tongue Press, 2000) and collected in *This Tremor Love Is* (Vancouver: Talonbooks, 2001).

"Here," from the chapbook sequence *here & there* (Lantzville, BC: Island Writing Series, 1981), was collected in *This Tremor Love Is*.

"This place full of contradiction," "Prairie," and "Kore" were published in *Touch to My Tongue* (Edmonton: Longspoon Press, 1984).

"Two women in a birth" and "Imagin-a-nation in the heart of" were published in *Double Negative,* by Daphne Marlatt and Betsy Warland (Charlottetown: gynergy books, 1988) and collected in *Two Women in a Birth,* by Daphne Marlatt and Betsy Warland (Toronto: Guernica Editions, 1994).

"There is a door" and "Shrimping" were published in *Salvage* (Red Deer: Red Deer College Press, 1991).

The selection from Nicole Brossard's *Mauve* was first published in *Mauve,* by Daphne Marlatt and Nicole Brossard (nbj/writing, 1985), and collected in *Salvage* (Red Deer: Red Deer College Press, 1991).

"Small print i, iii, v," "Booking passage," and "In the current" were published in *This Tremor Love Is* (Vancouver: Talonbooks, 2001).

"Generation, generations at the mouth" was published in *Steveston,* 3rd ed., with photographs by Robert Minden (Vancouver: Ronsdale Press, 2001).

Complicated" was published in *This Tremor Love Is* (Vancouver: Talonbooks, 2001).

"Years ago" was published in *The Gull,* with a Japanese translation by Toyoshi Yoshihara and a Preface by Richard Emmert (Vancouver: Talonbooks, 2009).

"Singing grass" was published in *Between Brush Strokes* (Saskatoon: JackPine Press, 2008).

"You remember" was published in *Seven Glass Bowls* (Vancouver: Nomados, 2003) and in *The Given* (Toronto: McClelland & Stewart, 2008).

"Walking" was published in *The Given* (Toronto: McClelland & Stewart, 2008).

"Tree-song" is from *Shadow Catch* (unpublished; produced by Pro Musica at Vancouver's Firehall Arts Centre, December 2010)).

"Spectacular," "To navigate," "Comes walking," "Marine, ah," and "Through cloud" were published in *Liquidities: Vancouver Poems Then and Now* (Vancouver: Talonbooks, 2013).

"Lift. step. drop" was first published in *The Capilano Review* 3, nos. 1 & 2 (2007) and then in *Prismatic Publics: Innovative Canadian Women's Poetry and Poetics,* ed. Kate Eichhorn and Heather Milne (Toronto: Coach House, 2009).

lps Books in the Laurier Poetry Series
Published by Wilfrid Laurier University Press

derek beaulieu *Please, No More Poetry: The Poetry of derek beaulieu,* edited by Kit Dobson, with an afterword by Lori Emerson • 2013 • xvi + 74 pp. • ISBN 978-1-55458-829-9

Dionne Brand *Fierce Departures: The Poetry of Dionne Brand,* edited by Leslie C. Sanders, with an afterword by Dionne Brand • 2009 • xvi + 44 pp. • ISBN 978-1-55458-038-5

Di Brandt *Speaking of Power: The Poetry of Di Brandt,* edited by Tanis MacDonald, with an afterword by Di Brandt • 2006 • xvi + 56 pp. • ISBN-10: 0-88920-506-x; ISBN-13: 978-0-88920-506-2

Nicole Brossard *Mobility of Light: The Poetry of Nicole Brossard,* edited by Louise H. Forsyth, with an afterword by Nicole Brossard • 2009 • xxvi + 118 pp. • ISBN 978-1-55458-047-7

George Elliott Clarke *Blues and Bliss: The Poetry of George Elliott Clarke,* edited by Jon Paul Fiorentino, with an afterword by George Elliott Clarke • 2008 • xviii + 72 pp. • ISBN 978-1-55458-060-6

Dennis Cooley *By Word of Mouth: The Poetry of Dennis Cooley,* edited by Nicole Markotić, with an afterword by Dennis Cooley • 2007 • xxii + 62 pp. • ISBN-10: 1-55458-007-2; ISBN-13: 978-1-55458-007-1

Lorna Crozier *Before the First Word: The Poetry of Lorna Crozier,* edited by Catherine Hunter, with an afterword by Lorna Crozier • 2005 • xviii + 62 pp. • ISBN-10: 0-88920-489-6; ISBN-13: 978-0-88920-489-8

Christopher Dewdney *Children of the Outer Dark: The Poetry of Christopher Dewdney,* edited by Karl E. Jirgens, with an afterword by Christopher Dewdney • 2007 • xviii + 60 pp. • ISBN-10: 0-88920-515-9; ISBN-13: 978-0-88920-515-4

Don Domanski *Earthly Pages: The Poetry of Don Domanski,* edited by Brian Bartlett, with an afterword by Don Domanski • 2007 • xvi + 62 pp. • ISBN-10: 1-55458-008-0; ISBN-13: 978-1-55458-008-8

Louis Dudek *All These Roads: The Poetry of Louis Dudek,* edited by Karis Shearer, with an afterword by Frank Davey • 2008 • xx + 70 pp. • ISBN 978-1-55458-039-2

George Fetherling *Plans Deranged by Time: The Poetry of George Fetherling,* edited by A.F. Moritz, with an afterword by George Fetherling • 2012 • xviii + 64 pp. • ISBN 978-1-55458-631-8

M. Travis Lane   *The Crisp Day Closing on My Hand: The Poetry of M. Travis Lane*, edited by Jeanette Lynes, with an afterword by M. Travis Lane • 2007 • xvi + 86 pp. • ISBN-10: 1-55458-025-0; ISBN-13: 978-1-55458-025-5

Tim Lilburn   *Desire Never Leaves: The Poetry of Tim Lilburn*, edited by Alison Calder, with an afterword by Tim Lilburn • 2007 • xiv + 50 pp. • ISBN-10: 0-88920-514-0; ISBN-13: 978-0-88920-514-7

Eli Mandel   *From Room to Room: The Poetry of Eli Mandel*, edited by Peter Webb, with an afterword by Andrew Stubbs • 2011 • xviii + 66 pp. • ISBN 978-1-55458-255-6

Daphne Marlatt   *Rivering: The Poetry of Daphne Marlatt*, edited by Susan Knutson, with an afterword by Daphne Marlatt • 2014 • xxiv + 72 pp. • ISBN 978-1-77112-038-8

Steve McCaffery   *Verse and Worse: Selected and New Poems of Steve McCaffery 1989–2009*, edited by Darren Wershler, with an afterword by Steve McCaffery • 2010 • xiv + 76 pp. • ISBN 978-1-55458-188-7

Don McKay   *Field Marks: The Poetry of Don McKay*, edited by Méira Cook, with an afterword by Don McKay • 2006 • xxvi + 60 pp. • ISBN-10: 0-88920-494-2; ISBN-13: 978-0-88920-494-2

Al Purdy   *The More Easily Kept Illusions: The Poetry of Al Purdy*, edited by Robert Budde, with an afterword by Russell Brown • 2006 • xvi + 80 pp. • ISBN-10: 0-88920-490-X; ISBN-13: 978-0-88920-490-4

F.R. Scott   *Leaving the Shade of the Middle Ground: The Poetry of F.R. Scott*, edited by Laura Moss, with an afterword by George Elliott Clarke • 2011 • xxiv + 72 pp. • ISBN 978-1-55458-367-6

Fred Wah   *The False Laws of Narrative: The Poetry of Fred Wah*, edited by Louis Cabri, with an afterword by Fred Wah • 2009 • xxiv + 78 pp. • ISBN 978-1-555458-046-0